anythink

D0772243

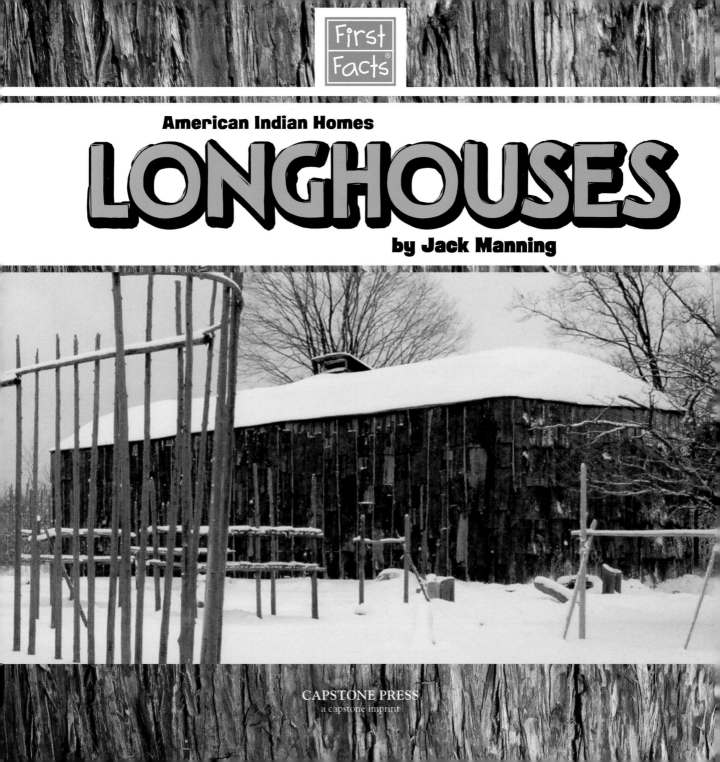

First Facts®

American Indian Homes

LONGHOUSES

by Jack Manning

CAPSTONE PRESS
a capstone imprint

First Facts are published by Capstone Press,
1710 Roe Crest Drive, North Mankato, Minnesota 56003
www.capstonepub.com

Library of Congress Cataloging-in-Publication Data
Manning, Jack.
  Longhouses / by Jack Manning.
     pages cm. — (First facts. American Indian homes)
  Includes bibliographical references and index.
  Summary: "Informative, engaging text and vivid photos introduce readers to longhouses"—
Provided by publisher.
  Audience: Grades K-3.
  ISBN 978-1-4914-0317-4 (library binding)
  ISBN 978-1-4914-0321-1 (paperback)
  ISBN 978-1-4914-0325-9 (eBook PDF)
1. Indians of North America—Dwellings. 2. Longhouses—North America. I. Title.
  E98.D9M25 2015
  728'.312—dc23   2014008072

Editorial Credits
Brenda Haugen, editor; Kyle Grenz, designer; Jo Miller, media researcher;
Kathy McColley, production specialist

Photo Credits
Alamy: North Wind Picture Archives, 19, Philip Scalia, 15; Bridgeman Art Library: Peter
Newark American Pictures/Private Collection, 17, Pitt Rivers Museum, Oxford, UK/Foster,
Horace (fl. 1870s), 21; Cartesia, 6 (map); Corbis: Nathan Benn, 9; Getty Images: Nativestock/
Marilyn Angel Wynn, 11; James P. Rowan, 7, 13; Shutterstock: Howard Sandler, 3, SF photo,
cover, 1, 5

Design Elements
Shutterstock: Joy Prescott, Tashatuvango

Printed in the United States of America in North Mankato, Minnesota.
032014   008087CGF14

Table of Contents

Chapter 1

What Is a Longhouse?

Longhouses are narrow wooden houses built by some American Indians. The houses have straight sides and curved roofs. Longhouses have doorways at each end but no windows.

The number of people living in a longhouse decided its length. Most houses were about 20 feet (6 meters) wide and 20 feet (6 m) tall. They were sometimes about 60 feet (18 m) long. Others were even longer.

Longhouses could be any length.

Chapter 2

Who Lived in a Longhouse?

Longhouses were the homes of some American Indians. They lived in what is now the northeastern United States and southeastern Canada. The Iroquois were the largest group of longhouse builders.

Up to 20 families could live in one longhouse. These families were part of a clan. They were all related through a woman called the clan mother.

Where the Iroquois Lived »

1. Canada
2. Lake Ontario
3. United States
4. Where the Iroquois lived
5. Atlantic Ocean

FACT

People don't live in longhouses anymore, but longhouses are still important. People use them for special gatherings.

clan—a large group of related families

7

Chapter 3

Gathering Materials

Materials to build longhouses were found in the forest. Men chopped down cedar and elm trees. Builders used this wood for the house's **frame**.

In late spring, Iroquois women peeled large sheets of bark from trees. They used the bark to cover the sides and roof of the longhouse.

FACT

The bark was easier to peel from the trees in late spring.

An Iroquois man dances in the snow outside a longhouse.

Chapter 4

Preparing the Materials

The Iroquois dried the sheets of bark. They put heavy stones on the sheets. The stones kept the bark flat until it was dry and ready to use.

The Iroquois also prepared other building materials. Some people cut strips of bark to make lacing. They used the lacing to tie sheets of bark to the frame. Other people cut pieces of wood into thick posts and thinner poles.

Sheets of bark are curly and need to be straightened.

FACT

People also made glue from deerskins. Builders used the glue to hold the wood poles together.

Chapter 5

Building a Longhouse

Builders chose a flat space to make a longhouse. They cleared the space of trees and brush. Then they set thick wood posts in the ground. The posts formed the outside walls. Builders tied poles to the outside walls of the longhouse. They bent the poles to make a dome roof. They covered the roof and sides of the longhouse with bark.

A longhouse frame was placed on a flat area.

Chapter 6

Inside a Longhouse

Each family had its own area in a longhouse. Families built platforms along the wall. People used these raised areas to work, sleep, and store food and supplies.

The Iroquois built fires in the center of the longhouse. Two families shared each fire. They used fires for cooking, heating, and light.

FACT

Longhouses had holes in the roof to let smoke escape.

Longhouses had places to cook, sleep, and store supplies.

Chapter 7

Longhouse Villages

The Iroquois built villages of various sizes. Some villages had just a few longhouses. Other villages had 200 homes.

A wall 20 feet (6 m) high circled each village. The **palisade** protected the village from enemies and wild animals.

The Iroquois moved about every 20 years and built new longhouses. They believed moving to a new place gave the earth time to rest.

> **palisade**—a tall fence that protected an Iroquois village from wind, animals, and enemy attacks

a 1651 Dutch map of longhouse villages

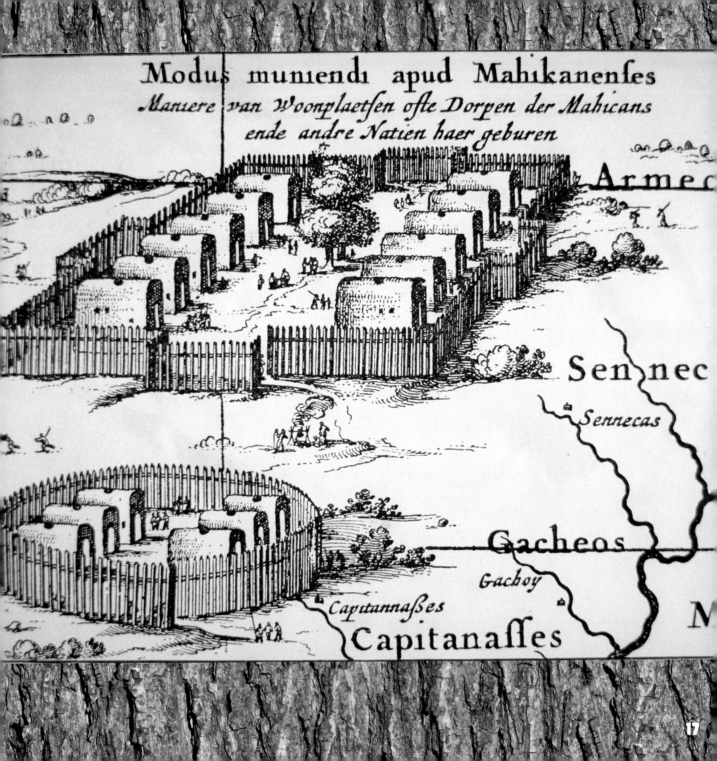

Modus muniendi apud Mahikanenses
Maniere van Woonplaetsen ofte Dorpen der Mahicans
ende andre Natien haer geburen

Armec

Sennec

Sennecas

Gacheos

Gachoy

Capitannaſſes

Capitanaſſes

M

Chapter 8

Special Longhouses

Each village had a special longhouse owned by the chief. The chief's home was a place to welcome visitors from other **nations**. Leaders met in the chief's house to talk. People in the village also came to this longhouse for **ceremonies**.

People built some longhouses as places to prepare food. They sometimes used longhouses to store food.

> **nation**—a tribe, or a group of people, who live in the same area and speak the same language
>
> **ceremony**—formal actions, words, and often music performed to mark an important occasion

a special ceremony in a longhouse

Some people still use longhouses for meetings and ceremonies.

A Special Symbol

The longhouse was the symbol of the Iroquois Confederacy. Nations making up this group were the Mohawk, Oneida, Seneca, Onondaga, and Cayuga. They believed they were like families in one large longhouse.

Amazing but True

Each longhouse had an aisle down the middle. This large open area was where children played and families cooked and ate. The aisle ran the entire length of the house. The bigger your family, the longer the aisle—and the house. Some longhouses were 300 feet (91 m) long. That's nearly as long as a football field!

a gathering of some of the Iroquois chiefs in 1871

symbol—an object that stands for something else

confederacy—a union of people or tribes with a common goal

aisle—a walkway between seats or living areas in a longhouse

Glossary

aisle (ILE)—a walkway between seats or living areas in a longhouse

ceremony (SER-uh-moh-nee)—formal actions, words, and often music performed to mark an important occasion

clan (KLAN)—a large group of related families

confederacy (kuhn-FED-ur-uh-see)—a union of people or tribes with a common goal

frame (FRAYM)—the basic shape over which a house is built

nation (NAY-shuhn)—a tribe, or a group of people, who live in the same area and speak the same language

palisade (pal-uh-SAYD)—a tall fence that protected an Iroquois village from wind, animals, and enemy attacks

symbol (SIM-buhl)—an object that stands for something else

Read More

Ditchfield, Christin. *Northeast Indians.* First Nations of North America. Chicago: Heinemann Library, 2012.

Dolbear, Emily J., and Peter Benoit. *The Iroquois.* A True Book. New York: Children's Press, 2011.

Tieck, Sarah. *Iroquois.* Native Americans. Edina, Minn.: ABDO Publishing Company, 2015.

Internet Sites

FactHound offers a safe, fun way to find Internet sites related to this book. All of the sites on FactHound have been researched by our staff.

Here's all you do:

Visit *www.facthound.com*

Type in this code: 9781491403174

Super-cool stuff! Check out projects, games and lots more at **www.capstonekids.com**

Index

Critical Thinking Using the Common Core

1. A chief had his own special longhouse. What made it special? Was it more than just a home? (Key Ideas and Details)

2. Look at the photo on page 15. What does it show? Would you like to live in a longhouse like this? Say why. (Integration of Knowledge and Ideas)